PowerKids Readers:

The Bilingual Library of the
United States of America™

Bilingual Edition
English/Spanish
Edición bilingüe

NEW MEXICO
NUEVO MÉXICO

JOSÉ MARÍA OBREGÓN

TRADUCCIÓN AL ESPAÑOL: MARÍA CRISTINA BRUSCA

The Rosen Publishing Group's
PowerKids Press™ & Editorial Buenas Letras™
New York

Published in 2006 by The Rosen Publishing Group, Inc.
29 East 21st Street, New York, NY 10010

First Edition

Book Design: Albert B. Hanner
Photo Credits: Cover © Craig Lovell/Corbis; p.p. 5, 31 (zia) © Joseph Sohm; Chromosohm Inc./Corbis; p.7 ©2002 © Geoatlas; p.p. 9, 30 (nickname) © Frank Lukasseck/Corbis; p.p. 11, 31 (cliff) © George H. H. Huey/Corbis; p.p. 13, 31 (Chavez) (Hanna) © Bettmann/Corbis; p. 15 © David Muench/Corbis; p. 17 Albert B. Hanner; p.p. 19, 21, 30 (motto) © Danny Lehman/Corbis; p.p. 23, 31 (microchip) © Roger DuBulsson/Corbis; p.p. 25, 30 (capital) © Mark E. Gibson/Corbis; p.p. 26, 30 (bird) © D. Robert & Lorri Franz/Corbis; p. 30 (state flower) © Theo Allofs/Corbis, (Tree) © Tom Bean/Corbis; p. 31 (Martinez) © Horace Bristol/Corbis, p. 31 (Denver) © Neal Preston/Corbis, (Gutierrez) National Aeronautics and Space Administration, (Moore) © Reuters/Corbis.

Library of Congress Cataloging-in-Publication Data

Obregón, José María, 1963–
New Mexico = Nuevo México / José María Obregón ; traducción al español, María Cristina Brusca. — 1st ed.
p. cm. – (The bilingual library of the United States of America) Includes bibliographical references and index.
ISBN 1-4042-3096-3 (library binding)
1. New Mexico—Juvenile literature.   I. Title. II. Title: Nuevo México. III. Series.
F796.3.O27 2006
978.9—dc22

2005016973

Manufactured in the United States of America

Due to the changing nature of Internet links, Editorial Buenas Letras has developed an online list of Web sites related to the subject of this book. This site is updated regularly. Please use this link to access the list:

http://www.buenasletraslinks.com/ls/newmexico

Contents

Contenido

Welcome to New Mexico

These are the flag and seal of the state of New Mexico. The flag has a red *zia* in the center. A *zia* is a Native American drawing that stands for the Sun.

Bienvenidos a Nuevo México

Estos son la bandera y el escudo de Nuevo México. La bandera tiene en el centro un símbolo *zía* de color rojo. El *zía* es un dibujo nativoamericano que representa un sol.

New Mexico Flag and State Seal

Bandera y escudo del estado de Nuevo México

New Mexico Geography

New Mexico borders the states of Arizona, Utah, Colorado, Oklahoma, and Texas. It also borders the country of Mexico. The Rio Grande runs from the north to the south of the state.

Geografía de Nuevo México

Nuevo México linda con los estados de Arizona, Utah, Colorado, Oklahoma y Texas. También linda con un país, México. El río Grande atraviesa el estado de norte a sur.

UTAH

COLORADO

ARIZONA

Farmington

Gallup **Los Alamos**

⭐ **Santa Fe**

Albuquerque

NEW MEXICO
NUEVO MÉXICO

Clovis

TEXAS

Socorro

Roswell

Pecos River
Río Pecos

Río Grande
Río Grande

Hobbs

Las Cruces

Carlsbad

Map Key
Claves del mapa

🔴 Major City
Ciudad principal

⭐ Capital
Capital

〰️ River
Río

MEXICO
MÉXICO

Map of New Mexico

Mapa de Nuevo México

The weather in New Mexico is usually warm and dry. The White Sands National Monument is a desert that covers 144,000 acres (58,277 ha).

El clima en Nuevo México es casi siempre caluroso y seco. El Monumento Nacional White Sands es un desierto que abarca 144,000 acres (58,277 ha).

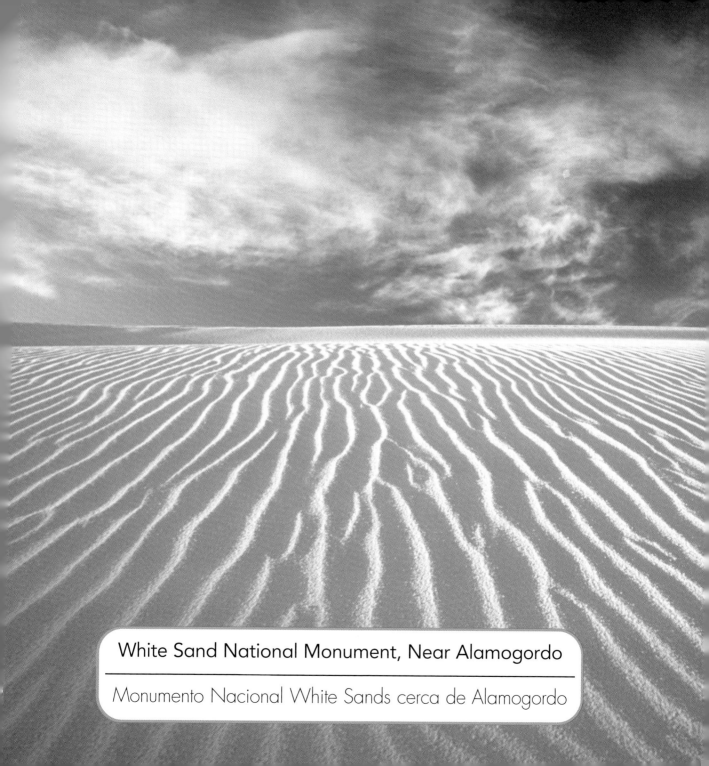

White Sand National Monument, Near Alamogordo

Monumento Nacional White Sands cerca de Alamogordo

New Mexico History

The Anasazi Indians lived in New Mexico from the eleventh century to the fourteenth century. The Anasazi built large villages called pueblos. Some pueblos were built on cliffs.

Historia de Nuevo México

La tribu Anasazi vivió en Nuevo México desde el siglo once hasta el siglo catorce. Los Anasazi construyeron grandes pueblos. Algunos pueblos fueron construídos en acantilados.

Anasazi Cliff Dwellings

Casas Anasazi en un acantilado

Juan Vásquez de Coronado was a Spanish explorer. He came to what is now New Mexico in 1540. Coronado was looking for the Seven Golden Cities of Cíbola. These cities were said to be made of gold.

Juan Vásquez de Coronado fue un explorador español. En 1540, llegó hasta lo que hoy es Nuevo México. Coronado estaba buscando las Siete Ciudades Doradas de Cíbola. Se decía que estas ciudades estaban hechas de oro.

Coronado on the Rio Grande

Coronado en el río Grande

The Spanish named the area New Mexico. In those days Mexico belonged to Spain. In 1821, Mexico won independence from Spain and New Mexico became part of Mexico. In 1848, New Mexico became part of the United States.

Los españoles llamaron Nuevo México a esta región. En esos días México pertenecía a España. En 1821, México se independizó de España y Nuevo México pasó a ser parte de México. En 1848, Nuevo México comenzó a formar parte de los Estados Unidos.

Mission San Miguel in Santa Fe, New Mexico

Misión San Miguel en Santa Fe, Nuevo México

Octaviano Larrazolo was the governor of New Mexico from 1919 to 1921. In 1928, Larrazolo became the first Hispanic in the U.S. Senate.

Octaviano Larrazolo fue gobernador de Nuevo México desde 1919 hasta 1921. En 1928, Larrazolo se convirtió en el primer hispano en el senado de los Estados Unidos.

Octaviano Larrazolo

Living in New Mexico

Almost 5 of every 10 people in New Mexico are Hispanic. This is more than in any other state. Hispanics are people that came to America from Spanish-speaking countries.

La vida en Nuevo México

Casi 5 de cada 10 habitantes de Nuevo México son hispanos. Esto es más que en cualquier otro estado. Los hispanos son personas que provienen de países en donde se habla el español.

Mexican Dancers

Bailarinas mexicanas

Santa Fe is the capital of New Mexico. Santa Fe calls itself "city different." The city has many buildings made of adobe. Adobes are bricks made of clay and straw and dried in the sun. Adobe is a Spanish word.

Santa Fe es la capital de Nuevo México. Santa Fe se llama a sí misma "ciudad única". La ciudad tiene muchos edificios de adobe. Los ladrillos de adobe están hechos de barro y paja, secados al sol.

Adobe Buildings in Santa Fe, New Mexico

Edificios de adobe en Santa Fe, Nuevo México

New Mexico Today

New Mexico is a leader in the production of microchips. Microchips are tiny pieces of electronics that make computers, cell phones, and other machines work.

Nuevo México, hoy

Nuevo México es líder en la fabricación de microprocesadores. Los microprocesadores son pequeñas piezas electrónicas que hacen funcionar a las computadoras, los teléfonos celulares y otras máquinas.

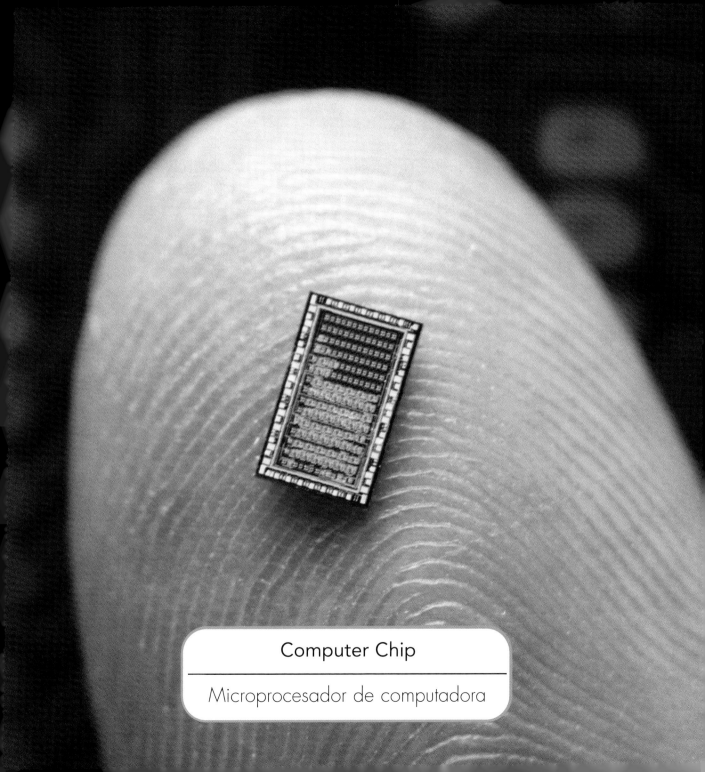

Computer Chip

Microprocesador de computadora

Albuquerque, Las Cruces, Santa Fe, Roswell, and Farmington are important cities in New Mexico. The New Mexico state capitol in Santa Fe is one of the newest capitol buildings in the country. It was built in 1966.

Albuquerque, Las Cruces, Santa Fe, Roswell y Farmington son ciudades importantes de Nuevo México. El capitolio del estado de Nuevo México es uno de los más nuevos del país. Fue construído en 1996.

New Mexico State Capitol

Capitolio del estado de Nuevo México

Activity:
Let´s Draw New Mexico's Bird

The roadrunner is a bird that would rather run than fly!

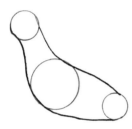

Actividad:
Dibujemos el ave de Nuevo México

¡El correcaminos es un ave que prefiere correr a volar!

1

Start by drawing three circles for the rough shape of the roadrunner. Connect your circles to form the shape of the bird's body.

Comienza por dibujar tres círculos. Luego, conecta los círculos para formar el cuerpo del ave.

2

Erase extra lines and smudges.

Borra las líneas innecesarias y perfecciona el contorno.

3

Add a triangle with a line down the center for the beak. Add another triangle for the tail and one for the wing.

Agrega un triángulo con una línea en el centro para hacer el pico. Traza otro triángulo para representar la cola y un triángulo más en el lugar del ala.

4

Erase extra lines. Draw the legs, the feet, and an eye.

Borra las líneas sobrantes. Dibuja las patas, los pies y el ojo.

5

Add shading and detail to your roadrunner.

Agrega sombras y detalles a tu correcaminos.

Timeline   Cronología

Pueblo Indians establish villages along the Rio Grande.	**A.D. 1200-1500**	Los indios Pueblo establecen poblaciones a lo largo del río Grande.
Francisco Vásquez de Coronado explores New Mexico.	**1540-1542**	Francisco Vásquez de Coronado explora Nuevo México.
Major gold discovery in Ortiz Mountains, south of Santa Fe.	**1828**	Gran descubrimiento de oro en las montañas Ortiz, al sur de Santa Fe.
Mexican-American War begins.	**1846**	Comienza la guerra entre México y los Estados Unidos.
New Mexico is admitted to the Union as the forty-seventh state.	**1912**	Nuevo México pasa a formar parte de la Unión como el estado cuarenta y siete.
Pancho Villa raids Columbus, New Mexico.	**1916**	Pancho Villa ataca e invade Columbus, Nuevo México.
The world's first atomic bomb is detonated in southern New Mexico.	**1945**	En el sur de Nuevo México se detona por primera vez en el mundo una bomba atómica.

New Mexico Events Eventos en Nuevo México

January
Winter Festival in Red River

April
Intertribal Powwow

May
Green Corn Dance at San Felipe Pueblo

May-June
Taos Spring Arts Celebration

June
New Mexico Arts and Crafts Fair in Albuquerque

August
Billy the Kid Pageant in Lincoln

September
Fiesta de Santa Fe
New Mexico State Fair in Albuquerque

October
Navajo Fair in Shiprock
International Balloon Fiesta in Albuquerque

December
Christmas Eve dances in mission churches at Indian pueblos

Enero
Festival de invierno, en Red River

Abril
Powwow Intertrubus

Mayo
Danza del maíz verde, en el Pueblo San Felipe

Mayo-Junio
Celebraciones de la primavera y el arte de Taos

Junio
Feria de arte y artesanías de Nuevo México, en Albuquerque

Agosto
Espectáculo Billy the Kid, en Lincoln

Septiembre
Fiesta de Santa Fe
Feria del estado de Nuevo México, en Albuquerque

Octubre
Feria Navajo, en Shiprock
Fiesta Internacional de globos aerostáticos en Albuquerque

Diciembre
Danzas de la Nochebuena en las iglesias de las misiones de los pueblos indios

29

New Mexico Facts/
Datos sobre Nuevo México

Population
1.8 million

Población
1.8 millones

Capital
Santa Fe

Capital
Santa Fe

State Motto
Crecit eundo, It grows as it goes

Lema del estado
Crecit eundo, Crecemos al andar

State Flower
Yucca

Flor del estado
Yuca

State Bird
Roadrunner

Ave del estado
Correcaminos

State Nickname
Land of Enchantment

Mote del estado
Tierra del Encanto

State Tree
Piñon

Árbol del estado
Pino piñonero

State Song
"O Fair New Mexico"

Canción del estado
"Oh, bello Nuevo México"

30

Famous New Mexicans/
Neomexicanos famosos

María Martinez
(1887–1980)

Potter
Ceramista

Dennis Chavez
(1888–1962)

Politician
Político

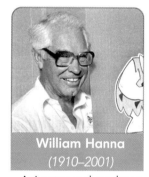

William Hanna
(1910–2001)

Animator and producer
Productor de cine de animación

John Denver
(1943–1997)

Singer and songwriter
Cantautor

Sid Gutierrez
(1951—)

Astronaut
Astronauta

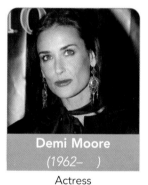

Demi Moore
(1962–)

Actress
Actriz

Words to Know/Palabras que debes saber

border
frontera

cliff
acantilado

microchip
microprocesador

zia
zía

Here are more books to read about New Mexico:
Otros libros que puedes leer sobre Nuevo México:

In English/En inglés:
New Mexico
America the Beautiful
by Kent, Deborah
Children's Press, 1999

In Spanish/En español:
Nuevo Mexico
World Almanac Biblioteca de los Estados
by Burgan, Michael
World Almanac Library, 2005

Words in English: 348

Palabras en español: 362

Index

Índice